Delaney
Street
Press

Love Is...

Love Is...

A Treasury of Timeless Quotations
About Matters of the Heart

Compiled and Edited by

Criswell Freeman

DELANEY STREET PRESS
Nashville, TN: (800) 256-8584

ISBN 1-58334-062-9

The ideas expressed in this book are not, in all cases, exact quotations, as some have been edited for clarity and brevity. In all cases, the author has attempted to maintain the speaker's original intent. In some cases, material for this book was obtained from secondary sources, primarily print media. While every effort was made to ensure the accuracy of these sources, the accuracy cannot be guaranteed. For additions, deletions, corrections or clarifications in future editions of this text, please write DELANEY STREET PRESS.

Printed in the United States of America
Cover Design by Bart Dawson
Typesetting & Page Layout by Sue Gerdes

1 2 3 4 5 6 7 8 9 10 • 00 01 02 03 04 05 06

ACKNOWLEDGMENTS

The author gratefully acknowledges the helpful support of Angela Beasley Freeman, Dick and Mary Freeman, Mary Susan Freeman, Jim Gallery, and the entire team of professionals at DELANEY STREET PRESS and WALNUT GROVE PRESS.

For Angela

Table of Contents

And now abideth
faith, hope, love,
these three; but the
greatest of these
is love.

I Corinthians 13:13

1

Love Is...

Love is many things: It is emotion; it is caring; it is cooperation; it is communication. Love is an exercise in both trust and trustworthiness. It provides a brief glimpse of eternity and a tiny taste of heaven.

Through the words of notable men and women, we examine various aspects of the little four-letter word that is simply too big to be explained by a single definition, or, for that matter, by a dozen definitions. That little word, of course, is love.

Love is the ultimate and the highest goal
to which man can aspire.
Viktor Frankl

Love is the most basic human need,
at the level of life at which human beings
are able to be human, because their
energies are not entirely absorbed
by the need to keep alive.
Rosemary Haughton

Love is the crowning grace of humanity,
the holiest right of the soul.
Petrarch

Love is the only gold.

Alfred, Lord Tennyson

Love is the river of life in this world.
Not until you have gone through the
rocky gorges, and not lost the stream;
not until you have gone through the
meadow, and the stream has widened and
deepened...not until you have come to
the unfathomable ocean, and poured your
treasures into its depths — not until then
can you know what love is.

Henry Ward Beecher

Love seeks one thing only: the good
of the one loved. It leaves all the other
secondary effects to take care of themselves. Love, therefore, is its own reward.

Thomas Merton

Love is not merely a contributor...
to meaningful life. In its own way it may
underlie all other forms of meaning.
Irving Singer

Love is ever the beginning of knowledge
as fire is of light.
Thomas Carlyle

The giving of love is an education in itself.
Eleanor Roosevelt

Love is the healer, the reconciler,
the inspirer, the creator....
Rosemary Haughton

Love is a game that two can play
and both win.
Eva Gabor

Love is the subtlest force
in the world.
Mohandas Gandhi

Love is the essence of God.

Ralph Waldo Emerson

Let love be purified, and all the rest
will follow. A pure love is thus, indeed,
the panacea for all the ills of the world.
Henry David Thoreau

Love is Nature's second sun.
George Chapman

Till it has loved, no man or woman
can become itself.
Emily Dickinson

Love is an irresistible desire
to be irresistibly desired.
Robert Frost

Love is union under the condition
of preserving one's integrity.
Erich Fromm

We are all born for love; it is
the principle of existence
and its only end.
Benjamin Disraeli

Love is a multiplication.

Marjory Stoneman Douglas

Love is the only sane
and satisfactory answer
to the problems of
human existence.

Erich Fromm

Real love is a permanently
  self-enlarging experience.
                                M. Scott Peck

A man is only as good as
  what he loves.
                                Saul Bellow

Inasmuch as love grows in you,
  so beauty grows. For love is
    the beauty of the soul.
                                St. Augustine

Love is a great beautifier.

Louisa May Alcott

Life is the flower
of which love
is the honey.

Victor Hugo

2

Love Is…An Emotion

The emotion of love is a life-altering experience. Once a man or woman loves deeply and sincerely, he or she is forever changed. The experience of intense emotional attachment to another human being is both joyful and fear-provoking: One's heart is filled with bliss, but one's head warns of the possibility that the state of bliss might be short-lived.

Genuine love moves, somehow, beyond the risk of loss, and loves for its own sake. Thus authentic, mature love supersedes all other human emotions because it permanently enlarges the heart of the man or woman who has experienced it.

The hope for permanent oneness is at the heart of romantic love.

Irving Singer

Love is trembling happiness.

Kahlil Gibran

Life's greatest happiness
is to be convinced
we are loved.

Victor Hugo

At the touch of love, everyone
becomes a poet.

Plato

If equal affection cannot be,
let the more loving be me.

W. H. Auden

Our soulmate is
the one who makes
life come to life.

Richard Bach

Whoever loves true life,
        will love true love.
                    Elizabeth Barrett Browning

For those passionately in love,
    the whole world seems to smile.
                    David Myers

Take away love and our earth
            is a tomb.
                    Robert Browning

One word frees us of all the weight
and pain of life: That word is love.
Sophocles

To love is to receive a glimpse of heaven.
Karen Sunde

As selfishness and complaint pervert
and cloud the mind, so love with its joys
clears and sharpens the vision.
Helen Keller

Love lives the moment; it's neither lost
in yesterday nor does it crave for tomorrow.
Love is now.

Leo Buscaglia

Bitterness imprisons life; love releases it.

Harry Emerson Fosdick

Love yourself first and everything else
falls into line. You really have to love
yourself to get anything done in this world.

Lucille Ball

We receive love not in proportion to our
demands or sacrifices or needs,
but roughly in proportion to our
own capacity to love.
Rollo May

Love, like death, changes everything.
Kahlil Gibran

Until I truly loved, I was alone.
Caroline Norton

The best and most
beautiful things in the
world cannot be seen
or even touched.
They must be felt
with the heart.

Helen Keller

Love stretches your heart and makes you big inside.

Margaret Walker

3

Love Is...A Choice

José Ortega y Gasset writes, "Love, in its very essence, is choice." His words remind us that love is much more than simply "falling" for another person. Love, at its core, is a conscious decision to commit oneself to another.

The emotions of love are sometimes fickle, but the decision to love doesn't waver. Authentic love is a committed, determined choice.

True love is not
a feeling by which
we are overwhelmed.
It is a committed,
thoughtful decision.

M. Scott Peck

Though people describe their experience
of falling in love as if it were a bolt
from the blue, this tempestuous event
is the outcome of a destiny they
have chosen for themselves.

Irving Singer

Love is an activity, not a passive affect;
it is a "standing in," not a "falling for."

Erich Fromm

Love is an active verb —
a river, not a pond.

Robert Fulghum

There is no love where there is no will.
Mohandas Gandhi

Love is an act of will — namely, both
an intention and an action. Will also
implies choice. We do not have to love.
We choose to love.
M. Scott Peck

Love is not only
something you feel.
It's something you do.

David Wilkerson

Love doesn't just sit there, like stone; it has to be made, like bread, remade all the time, made new.

Ursula K. LeGuin

Love must be learned again and again;
there is no end to it.
Hate needs no instruction.
Katherine Anne Porter

As passions subside after the initial
infatuation, dedication to each other's
welfare and happiness emerge as the
major binding forces in a relationship.
Aaron Beck

Loving is something more serious and
significant than being excited by the lines
of a face and the color of a cheek.
It is a decision.
José Ortega y Gasset

One does not fall "in"
or "out" of love.
One grows in love.

Leo Buscaglia

Neither a lofty degree of intelligence
nor imagination nor both together go to
the making of genius. Love, love, love,
that is the soul of genius.
Wolfgang Amadeus Mozart

If one wishes to know love,
one must live love, in action.
Leo Buscaglia

We can only learn to love by loving.
Iris Murdoch

Let my heart be wise. It is the gods' best gift.

Euripides

4

Love Is...Trust

Trust is the foundation of love upon which everything else is built. Absent trust, a love quickly withers, for no relationship can flourish in an atmosphere of jealousy and fear. But with enough trust, love can last a lifetime — and beyond.

Love is trusting.

Leo Buscaglia

The best proof of love is trust.
Dr. Joyce Brothers

Where love is, there is faith.
Where there is no trust,
there is no love.
Ellen Royals

The sincerity of the commitments
are tested by the faithfulness
of the lover.
Vincent Brümmer

Love is responsibility.

Martin Buber

Love requires trust in the fidelity
of another.
Arthur D. Colman and Libby Lee Colman

There is no panic in trust.
Bertha Munro

Trust begets truth.
William Gurney Benham

The jealous person engenders the very
thing he fears: the withdrawal of love.
Viktor Frankl

The jealous are troublesome to others,
but a torment to themselves.
William Penn

In jealousy there is more of self-love
than love.
La Rochefoucauld

It is not love that produces jealousy —
it is selfishness.

Justice Wallington

It is true that selfish persons are incapable
of loving others, but they are not capable
of loving themselves either.

Erich Fromm

Love will not always linger longest
With those who hold it in
too clenched a fist.

Alice Duer Miller

Few delights can equal the mere presence
of one whom we trust utterly.
George MacDonald

Without trust, the mind's lot
is a hard one.
Bettina von Arnim

How desperately we wish to maintain
our trust in those we love! In the face of
everything, we try to find reasons to trust.
Because losing faith is worse than
falling out of love.
Sonia Johnson

To be trusted is
a greater compliment
than to be loved.

George MacDonald

Knit your hearts with an unslipping knot.

William Shakespeare

5

Love Is...Kindness

For love to be anything but superficial, words must be translated into deeds. The words "I love you" take only a moment to speak, but they take a lifetime to demonstrate. Ultimately, our actions —not our words— are the true expressions of our feelings. Acts of consideration and kindness, performed consistently and over a long period of time, are the ultimate proof of mature love.

Love is patient, love is kind....

I Corinthians 13:4

Love is shown by deeds, not by words.
Philippine Proverb

Love is not just some great abstract
idea or feeling. There are some people
with such a lofty conception of love that
they never succeed in expressing it in the
simple kindnesses of ordinary life.
Paul Tournier

The best portion of a good man's life
is his little, nameless, unremembered acts
of kindness and of love.
William Wordsworth

There is no love which does not become help.

Paul Tillich

There is but one genuine love potion —
consideration.

Menander

If you'd be loved, be worthy to be loved.

Ovid

Never let your willingness grow dim, let
the spirit of love light up your whole life,
as you hold yourselves at the service
of love.

Paul of Tarsus

Kind words can be
short and easy to speak,
but their echoes are
truly endless.

Mother Teresa

Kindness is the language which the deaf can hear and the blind can see.
Mark Twain

The more one judges, the less one loves.
Honoré de Balzac

Love never dies of starvation, but often of indigestion.
Ninon de Lenclos

Love is my decision to make
your problem my problem.
Robert Schuller

Accustom yourself continually to make
many acts of love, for they enkindle
and melt the soul.
St. Teresa of Avila

Tenderness and kindness are not signs of
weakness and despair but manifestations
of strength and resolution.
Kahlil Gibran

All love that has not friendship
for its base is like a mansion built
upon the sand.
Ella Wheeler Wilcox

He who sows courtesy reaps
friendship, and he who plants
kindness gathers love.
Saint Basil

Couples who play together
stay together.
Paul Pearsall

Life is an exciting
business and most
exciting when lived
for other people.

Helen Keller

The strongest evidence
of love is sacrifice.

Carolyn Fry

The older you get, the
more you realize that
kindness is synonymous
with happiness.

Lionel Barrymore

6

Love Is...Communication

Falling in love can occur with remarkably little in the way of verbal interchange. Staying in love, on the other hand, usually requires clear, consistent, continuous communication. Couples who learn to share their innermost hopes, fears, dreams, and opinions will reap powerful rewards, as the following quotations clearly attest.

I like not only to be
loved, but to be told
I am loved.

George Eliot

Good communication
is as stimulating as
black coffee and just
as hard to sleep after.

Anne Morrow Lindbergh

Love is living the experience of another
person in all his uniqueness
and singularity.
Viktor Frankl

Love is a mutual self-giving which ends
in self-recovery.
Bishop Fulton J. Sheen

Love involves a peculiar unfathomable
combination of understanding
and misunderstanding.
Diane Arbus

The first duty of love
is to listen.

Paul Tillich

Life is a romantic business, but you have to make the romance.

Oliver Wendell Holmes, Sr.

Perhaps love is the
process of my leading
you gently back
to yourself.

Antoine de Saint-Exupéry

There are never enough
"I love you"s.

Lenny Bruce

7

Love Is...Sharing

Successful couples learn to share many things: hopes, dreams, possessions, encouragement, laughter, trust, responsibilities, opinions, fears, tears, time, and most of all love. On the pages that follow, wise men and women share common-sense advice for successfully sharing love — and life.

Love is, above all, the gift of oneself.

Jean Anouilh

To get the full value
of joy, you have to have
someone to divide
it with.

Mark Twain

Love gives itself; it is not bought.
Henry Wadsworth Longfellow

The love we give away is the only love
we keep.
Elbert Hubbard

Discover someone to help shoulder
your misfortunes. Then, you will never
be alone. Neither fate, nor the crowd,
so readily attacks two.
Baltasar Gracián

To love at all is to be vulnerable.

C. S. Lewis

Mutual vulnerability is one of
the great gifts of love.

Thomas Moore

The one thing we can never get enough
of is love. And the one thing we
never give enough of is love.

Henry Miller

To be loved, love.

Decimus Maximus Ausonius

Love is primarily giving,
        not receiving.

Erich Fromm

Love is not getting but giving.

Henry Van Dyke

Love that is not freely given
      is not love at all.

Vincent Brümmer

Love is an act of endless forgiveness,
a tender look which becomes a habit.
Peter Ustinov

Love, and you shall be loved. All love
is mathematical, just as much as the two
sides of an algebraic equation.
Ralph Waldo Emerson

Love is the child of freedom,
never that of domination.
Erich Fromm

A wise lover values
not so much the gift
of the lover as the love
of the giver.

Thomas à Kempis

Unshared joy is an unlit candle.
Spanish Proverb

We cannot live only for ourselves.
A thousand fibers connect us
to our fellow man.
Herman Melville

Think as little as possible about yourself
and as much as possible
about other people.
Eleanor Roosevelt

Every charitable act is a stepping stone
toward heaven.

Henry Ward Beecher

The greatest good you can do for another
is not just to share your riches
but to reveal to him his own.

Benjamin Disraeli

What do we live for, if it is not to make
life less difficult for each other?

George Eliot

Ideally, couples need three lives: one for him, one for her, and one for them together.

Jacqueline Bisset

8

Love Is...Cooperation

Marcus Aurelius Antoninus writes, "We are born for cooperation, as are the feet, the hands, and the eyes." And so it is for lovers who, if they are to flourish, must first learn the subtle art of cooperation.

When two people decide to build a life together, they embark upon an adventure in compromise. The following quotations demonstrate the wisdom of working together in love.

Each partner should
take full responsibility
for improving
the relationship.

Aaron Beck

Love does not
dominate;
it cultivates.

Goethe

One hand cannot applaud alone.
Arabian Proverb

We must learn to work together
or we will not work at all.
Dwight D. Eisenhower

Coming together is a beginning;
keeping together is progress;
working together is success.
Henry Ford

Joint undertakings
stand a better chance
when they benefit
both sides.

Euripides

Everyone needs help from everyone.
Bertolt Brecht

An act of goodness is of itself an act
of happiness.
Maurice Maeterlinck

Be happy, because love gives us hope;
be patient in times of trouble, keep on
wanting the victory of love.
Paul of Tarsus

Hearts are not had as a gift
but hearts are earned....
William Butler Yeats

The greatest happiness in the world
is to make others happy.
Luther Burbank

It is enough that I am of value
to somebody today.
Hugh Prather

Your spouse is your closest relative and is entitled to depend on you as a common ally, supporter, and champion.

Aaron Beck

9

Love Is...Forever

Henry Van Dyke observed, "For those who love...time is eternity...." Van Dyke understood that the bonds of true love are not constrained by time or place. Real love endures, even outliving the lovers.

Love permanently changes people and, in doing so, the world. The echoes of a loving word, a compassionate deed, or a kind thought last forever.

If a thing loves, it is infinite.

William Blake

True love doesn't have a happy ending; true love doesn't have an ending.

Unknown

In dreams and in love
    there are no impossibilities.
Janos Arnay

The best way to know God
    is to love many things.
Vincent van Gogh

He who is filled with love is filled
    with God Himself.
St. Augustine

Nothing we do,
however virtuous, can be
accomplished alone;
therefore we are
saved by love.

Reinhold Niebuhr

When you come right
down to it, the secret
of having it all
is loving it all.

Dr. Joyce Brothers

The deepest truth blooms only
from the deepest love.
Heinrich Heine

The way to love anything is to realize
that it might be lost.
G. K. Chesterton

Love may not last forever but it lingers.
Robert Fulghum

There is a land of the living and a land of the dead and the bridge is love, the only survival, the only meaning.

Thornton Wilder

There is only
one terminal dignity —
love.

Helen Hayes

Love dies only
when growth stops.

Pearl Buck

Those who love deeply
never grow old; they
may die of old age,
but they die young.

Sir Arthur Wing Pinero

One can only obey the great law of the heart that says, "As long as you live, love one another and take the consequences."
Robert Fulghum

To cheat oneself out of love
is the most terrible deception.
Kierkegaard

When love and skill work together, expect a masterpiece.

John Ruskin

If you love life, life will love you back.

Artur Rubinstein

Love is the everlasting possession of the good.

Plato

The story of a love
is not important —
what is important is
that one is capable of
love. It is perhaps the
only glimpse we are
permitted of eternity.

Helen Hayes

Sources

About the Author

Criswell Freeman is a Doctor of Clinical Psychology living in Nashville, Tennessee. In addition to this text, Dr. Freeman is also the author of many other books, including his bestselling self-help book *When Life Throws You a Curveball, Hit It.*

About
DELANEY STREET PRESS

DELANEY STREET PRESS publishes books designed to inspire and entertain readers of all ages. DELANEY STREET books are distributed by WALNUT GROVE PRESS. For more information, call 1-800-256-8584.